Meals Around the World

Meals in China

by R.J. Bailey

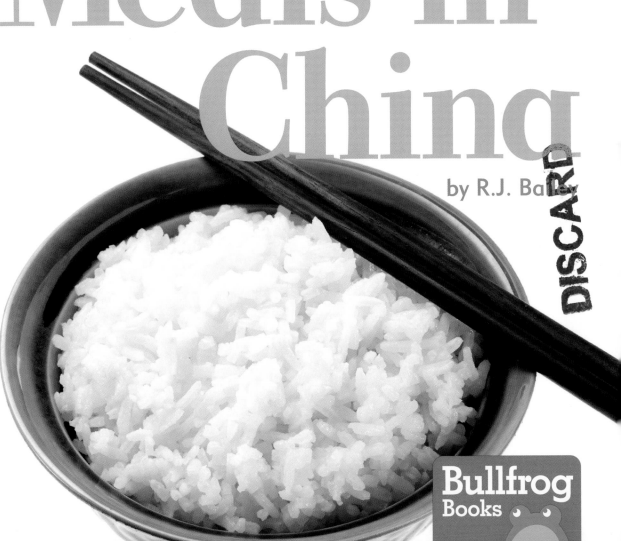

Bullfrog Books

Ideas for Parents and Teachers

Bullfrog Books let children practice reading informational text at the earliest reading levels. Repetition, familiar words, and photo labels support early readers.

Before Reading

- Discuss the cover photo. What does it tell them?
- Look at the picture glossary together. Read and discuss the words.

Read the Book

- "Walk" through the book and look at the photos. Let the child ask questions. Point out the photo labels.
- Read the book to the child, or have him or her read independently.

After Reading

- Prompt the child to think more. Ask: Have you ever eaten Chinese food? Were the flavors new to you? What did you like best?

Bullfrog Books are published by Jump!
5357 Penn Avenue South
Minneapolis, MN 55419
www.jumplibrary.com

Library of Congress Cataloging-in-Publication Data

Names: Bailey, R.J., author.
Title: Meals in China / by R.J. Bailey.
Description: Minneapolis, Minnesota: Jump!, Inc. [2017] | Series: Meals around the world
Audience: Ages 5–8. | Audience: K to grade 3.
Includes index.
Identifiers: LCCN 2016013093 (print)
LCCN 2016013591 (ebook)
ISBN 9781620313718 (hardcover: alk. paper)
ISBN 9781620314890 (pbk.)
ISBN 9781624964183 (ebook)
Subjects: LCSH: Food—China—Juvenile literature.
Cooking, Chinese—Juvenile literature.
Food habits—China—Juvenile literature.
Classification: LCC TX724.5.C5 B34 2017 (print)
LCC TX724.5.C5 (ebook) | DDC 394.1/20951—dc23
LC record available at http://lccn.loc.gov/2016013093

Editor: Jenny Fretland VanVoorst
Series Designer: Ellen Huber
Book Designer: Leah Sanders
Photo Researcher: Kirsten Chang

Photo Credits: All photos by Shutterstock except:
Alamy, 13; Getty, 4, 6–7, 9, 16–17, 19, 20–21, 22;
Purple-Gecko/Shutterstock.com, 23mr; Thinkstock, 1.

Printed in the United States of America at Corporate Graphics in North Mankato, Minnesota.

Table of Contents

Cooking in China

Wake up, Li!

It is morning in China.
Time for breakfast!

Li helps Mama cook.
Her sister helps, too.
What do they make?
Steamed buns.

What is inside?
Vegetables.
Some have meat.

Li drinks soy milk.

Now she is ready for school.

9

We break for lunch.

Mei eats rice.

She uses chopsticks.

Bao eats soup.
It has noodles in it.
After lunch, we nap.

Wei walks home.

He wants a snack.

Wow! What is that smell?

Stinky tofu.

It is fried street food.

It is time for dinner.

Mama cooks a duck.

She puts sauce on it.

She wraps it
in a pancake.

PoPo puts out cookies.
Yum!

She drinks tea.

It is hot.

We love eating with family!

Make Noodle Soup!

Make Chinese Noodle Soup! Be sure to get an adult to help. Serves two.

Ingredients:

- 4 cups chicken stock
- 2–3 green onions, sliced thin
- 1 tablespoon oyster sauce
- 2 tablespoons soy sauce
- 4 ounces dried Chinese noodles
- 4 bok choy leaves, sliced

Directions:

❶ In a large saucepan, bring chicken stock to a boil.
❷ Add the green onions, bok choy leaves, oyster sauce, soy sauce, and dried noodles.
❸ Turn the heat down; cook noodles until they are soft.
❹ Serve hot. Enjoy!

Picture Glossary

China
A country in Asia.

soy milk
Milk made by soaking dried soybeans and grinding them in water.

chopsticks
Two thin sticks of wood or plastic that you hold in one hand and use to eat food.

street food
Food made and sold by vendors on a street or in public.

PoPo
A name some Chinese children call their grandmother.

tofu
A soft food product made from soybean milk.

Index

To Learn More

Learning more is as easy as 1, 2, 3.

1) Go to www.factsurfer.com

2) Enter "mealsinChina" into the search box.

3) Click the "Surf" button to see a list of websites.

With factsurfer.com, finding more information is just a click away.